GA

CENGAGE Learning

Short Stories for Students, Volume 1

Staff

Kathleen Wilson, *Editor*

Tim Akers, Pamela S. Dear, David M. Galens, Jeffrey W. Hunter, Dan Jones, John D. Jorgenson, Marie Lazzari,
Jerry Moore, Deborah A. Stanley, Diane Telgen, Polly Vedder, Thomas Wiloch, *Contributing Editors*

Jeff Chapman, *Programmer/Analyst*

Greg Barnhisel, Stephan Dziemianowicz, Tim Engles, Mary Beth Folia, Christopher Giroux, Cynthia Hallett, Karen
Holleran, Jennifer Hicks, Logan Hill, Heidi Johnson, Tamara Kendig, David Kippen, Maryanne Kocis, Rena Korb,
Kim Long, Harvey Lynch, Thomas March, Carl Mowery, Robert Peltier, Elisabeth Piedmont-Marton, Trudy Ring,

Judy Sobeloff, Michael Sonkowsky, Anne Trubek, Julianne White, Janet Witalec, *Contributing Writers*

Susan Trosky, *Permissions Manager*
Kim Smilay, *Permissions Specialist*
Sarah Chesney, *Permissions Associate*
Steve Cusack, Kelly A. Quin, *Permissions Assistants*

Victoria Cariappa, *Research Team Leader*
Michele LaMeau, Barbara McNeil, Maureen Richards, *Research Specialists*
Laura C. Bissey, Julia C. Daniel, Tamara C. Nott, Tracie Richardson,
Norma Sawaya, Cheryl L. Warnock, *Research Associates*

Mary Beth Trimper, *Production Director*
Shanna Heilveil, *Production Assistant*

Cynthia Baldwin, *Production Design Manager*
Pamela A. E. Galbreath, *Senior Art Director*

Barbara J. Yarrow, *Graphic Services Manager*
Pamela Reed, *Photography Coordinator*
Randy Bassett, *Image Database Supervisor*

and inclusion in the publication of any organization, agency, institution, publication, service, or individual does not imply endorsement of the editors or publisher. Errors brought to the attention of the publisher and verified to the satisfaction of the publisher will be corrected in future editions.

Copyright © 1997
Gale Research
835 Penobscot Building
Detroit, MI 48226-4094

This book is printed on acid-free paper that meets the minimum requirements of American National Standard for Information Sciences-Permanence Paper for Printed Library Materials, ANSI Z39.48-1984.

ISBN 0-7876-1690-7
ISSN 1092-7735

Printed in the United States of America.
10 9 8 7 6 5 4 3 2

Young Goodman Brown

Nathaniel Hawthorne

1835

Introduction

"Young Goodman Brown," written in 1835 by Nathaniel Hawthorne, is known for being one of literature's most gripping portrayals of seventeenth-century Puritan society. The tale first appeared in the April issue of *New England Magazine* and was later included in Hawthorne's popular short story collection, *Mosses from an Old Manse*, in 1846.

"Young Goodman Brown" tells the tale of a young Puritan man drawn into a covenant with the Devil. Brown's illusions about the goodness of his society are crushed when he discovers that many of his fellow townspeople, including religious leaders and his wife, are attending a Black Mass. At the end of the story, it is not clear whether Brown's experience was nightmare or reality, but the results are nonetheless the same. Brown is unable to forgive the possibility of evil in his loved ones and as a result spends the rest of his life in desperate loneliness and gloom.

Though a work of fiction, "Young Goodman Brown" is widely considered to be one of the most effective literary works to address the hysteria surrounding the Salem Witch Trials of 1692. Hawthorne is also remembered for helping to establish the short story as a respected form of literature and as a proponent of instilling morals and lessons into his writing.

Author Biography

Hawthorne was an American fiction writer best known for his novel *The Scarlet Letter*. Born in Salem, Massachusetts, in 1804, he was one of those rare writers who drew critical acclaim during his lifetime. Today, readers still appreciate Hawthorne's work for its storytelling qualities and for the moral and theological questions it raises.

Throughout his lifetime, Hawthorne felt guilt over certain actions of his ancestors. Critics view his literary preoccupation with Puritanism as an outgrowth of these roots. The first Hawthorne to immigrate to Massachusetts from England was William, a magistrate who once ordered the public whipping of a Quaker woman. Shortly thereafter, William's son, John, served as a judge in the Salem witch trials of 1692. Hawthorne's own father was a ship's captain who died when Hawthorne was only four years old. As a result of his family history, Hawthorne filled much of his work, including "Young Goodman Brown," with themes exploring the evil actions of humans and the idea of original sin.

After graduating from Bowdoin College in Brunsick, Maine, in 1825, Hawthorne moved back to Salem where he lived with his mother and served a twelve-year literary apprenticeship. Though he wrote regularly, he destroyed most of his early work. Only the unsuccessful *Fanshawe* was published in 1828. Hawthorne later sought out and burned every available copy. It was during this bout of obscurity and insecurity that Hawthorne first published "Young Goodman Brown." Critics have since recognized it as one of his most successful short stories. In 1846 Hawthorne published it again as part of a collection of stories titled *Mosses from an Old Manse*.

Hawthorne married Sophia Peabody, a neighbor who admired his work, in 1842. The couple had two daughters and a son. In their first year of marriage they moved to the Old Manse in Concord, Massachusetts, a community known for its liberal atmosphere and for being the home of other several other famous writers and philosophers. Hawthorne worked diligently there for three straight years, producing *American Notebooks* and the essay "The Old Manse." He later described this period as the happiest of his life.

Family debts forced Hawthorne and his family to move back to Salem in 1945, where he filled the first of two presidentially-appointed posts. Under James K. Polk, he served as Custom House surveyor, but was discharged four years later by the Whig Administration. After losing his job, Hawthorne wrote *The Scarlet Letter*. Controversy surrounding his discharge, and the content of the book itself, boosted sales. In 1851, the Hawthornes moved back to Concord, where they purchased and remodeled the childhood homestead of Louisa May Alcott, the author of *Little Women*.

When his college friend Franklin Pierce was

elected president in 1853, Hawthorne was offered the U.S. Consulship to Liverpool, England. That term ended in 1857, and he and his family moved again, this time to a seaside village in England where Hawthorne wrote *The Marble Faun*, a book about his experiences abroad. During the last four years of his life, Hawthorne's health failed. He did write a well-received collection of essays titled *Our Old Home*, but his passion for writing faded. Hawthorne died in Plymouth, New Hampshire, in 1864, at the age of 59.

Plot Summary

"Young Goodman Brown" opens with Young Goodman Brown about to embark on an evening's journey. His young wife, Faith, fearful for some unknown reason, beseeches him to delay his journey. Goodman Brown, however, stresses that he has a task that must be accomplished before sunrise, and so the newlyweds reluctantly part. As he walks down the street, Goodman Brown chides himself for leaving Faith while he goes on his journey and resolves that, after this night, he will stay by the side of his good and pious wife. Pleased with himself, Goodman Brown then hurries through the forest to accomplish some unknown task.

Deeper in the forest Goodman Brown spies an old man, who is actually the Devil in disguise, waiting for him. Goodman Brown blames Faith for making him late. The older man, who has a curious resemblance to Goodman Brown, carries a staff which resembles a black snake. When the older man urges Goodman Brown to take the staff to ease his walk, Goodman Brown expresses second thoughts and his intention to go home. The older man convinces Goodman Brown to walk with him, however, and listen to the reasons why he should continue. Goodman Brown agrees and murmurs that his forefathers, good honest Christians, would never go on such a walk.

To his surprise, Brown finds this is not true.

His companion tells him that he is well acquainted with the Brown family and that he helped Brown's father and grandfather commit acts such as the punishment of religious dissenters and the massacre of Indians. While Goodman Brown expresses surprise, his companion continues to speak of the good Christians of New England with whom he is acquainted: deacons, town leaders, even the governor. Goodman Brown is amazed but tells his companion that were he to continue on this journey, he still would not be able to meet the eye of his minister. Hearing this, the older man breaks into a fit of laughter.

The two men then see Goody Cloyse, the old woman who serves as Goodman Brown's moral adviser. Not wanting to explain who he is with and where he is going, Goodman Brown hides in the woods. Again, Goodman Brown is surprised; the woman knows his companion, who has now taken on the appearance of Goodman Brown's grandfather. The two older people talk of a witch's recipe and the meeting that will take place this evening. Goodman Brown realizes that Goody Cloyse is a witch.

The two men continue walking through the forest. At a hollow in the road, Goodman Brown refuses to go any further, declaring he would rather be on the side of Faith than Goody Cloyse. His companion leaves him to think over the matter. Goodman Brown realizes that his decision to stop will enable him to meet his minister and deacon with a clear conscience. As he continues these comforting meditations, a carriage passes by on the road. Two men, who reveal themselves to be the minister and the deacon, speak of the evening's meeting and the young woman who will be joining. After the carriage has passed, Goodman Brown feels faint as he realizes that these men, too, are in communion with the Devil. Now he questions whether or not heaven really exists. Yet his love for Faith gives him the willpower to resist going to the meeting.

While he is lifting his hands to pray, however, he hears Faith's voice. He calls out for her, and she answers with a scream. He realizes that Faith is going to the meeting, and he decides to attend the meeting too because all good is now gone. Soon he reaches a clearing with a crude altar surrounded by the "saints" and "sinners" of Salem. While the Devil's congregation sings an evil hymn rejoicing in sin, Brown waits, hoping that he can find Faith. At a call for the new members he steps forward, and Faith is led forward by two women. A dark figure speaks of sin. He commands the newlyweds to look at each other and then declares that they now know virtue is but a dream and evil is the nature of mankind. Goodman Brown cries out to Faith to resist this evil.

He never finds out, however, if Faith does resist. As soon as the words are out of his mouth, Goodman Brown finds himself alone in the forest. The next morning he returns to Salem. Everywhere he goes he sees people who attended the meeting, but he turns away from them. He even turns from

Faith.

Though Goodman Brown never finds out whether or not he dreamed the meeting in the forest, the experience still has a profound effect on him. After that night, he becomes a stern, sad, and distrustful man. He rejects the faith he once had in his religion and even rejects his own wife. At his death, no hopeful words are carved upon his tombstone. He has lived a life of gloom, seeing sinners and blasphemers everywhere he looked.

Faith Brown

Faith Brown serves an allegorical purpose in this story. It is Faith that Brown leaves behind, presumably for one night, in order to keep his appointment with the Devil. Explaining to the old man why he is late Brown says, "Faith kept me back a while." She represents the force of good in the world. Thus, when Brown perceives that she too has been corrupted, he shouts "My Faith is gone!" and rushes madly toward the witches's gathering.

The pink ribbons that decorate Faith's cap have drawn more critical attention than any other symbol in the story. On one hand they have been said to represent female sexuality, while on the other, innocence. Or, they may merely signify the ornament of a sweet and cheerful wife. Whatever their purpose, Faith's pink ribbons are integral to the story's structure. They are mentioned three times: at the beginning when Brown is leaving Faith behind, near the climax when Brown sees a pink ribbon floating down from the heavens, and at the end when Brown is greeted by his wife upon his return.

Young Goodman Brown

Much of this story's extensive body of

criticism centers on its title character, whose name suggests he represents the average man. Brown makes his journey into the dark forest because he is curious and even tempted by the darker side of life. His brush with evil, however, leaves a permanently negative mark. Critics agree that whether the Black Mass really occurred or was dreamed, the impression on Brown is very real indeed.

At the beginning of the story, Brown appears confident in his ability to choose between good and evil, but once he stands before the Devil's altar, he can no longer believe that good always prevails. He becomes a profoundly disillusioned man, who sees wickedness everywhere, even in those closest to him. Some critics have interpreted Brown's resulting distrust and isolation as the result of a guilty conscience; he cannot forgive himself or others for hidden sinfulness. In the end, Brown is unable to accept the duality of human nature-that a person can possess both good and evil qualities—and for this he suffers.

The Devil

The figure of the Devil in "Young Goodman Brown" appears as an older—though not ancient—man who carries a twisted, snake-like staff. He seems to resemble Brown somewhat, and it has been suggested that he is a reflection of the darker side of Brown's nature. The Devil claims to know both Brown's grandfather, who participated in the persecution of Quakers, and Brown's father, who took part in an attack on an Indian village. Similar evil deeds were perpetrated in real life by Hawthorne's ancestors, and the author's alignment of his forefathers with the Devil suggests his feelings of guilt concerning his family history.

Media Adaptations

- In 1968, Edward J. Megroth adapted *Young Goodman Brown* as an opera, with music by Harold Fink.

- *Young Goodman Brown* was adapted as a motion picture by Pyramid Films in 1972. This thirty-minute film won a special jury award at the Atlanta International Film Festival.

Goody Cloyse, the Minister, and

Deacon Gookin

All three of these characters serve as dramatic examples of the wickedness and hypocrisy that may hide in the souls of those who appear most virtuous. These three are distinguished from among the crowd of townsfolk at the gathering because they represent a standard of piety and godliness that is destroyed for Brown by his experience. Both Goody Cloyse and Deacon Gookin were real people who were involved in the Salem Witch Trials of 1692.

Themes

"Young Goodman Brown" tells the story of a Puritan man who loses faith in humankind after he thinks he witnesses his wife and respected members of his town participating in a Black Mass. His experience dooms him to a life of gloom and mistrust.

Topics for Further Study

- What does Goodman Brown mean when he says, "Faith kept me back a while," after the Devil comments on his lack of punctuality?

- Was Goodman Brown's brush with evil real or imagined? Read other works of literature in which the line between reality and imagination is blurred, such as "The Swimmer" by John Cheever and "The Fall of the House of Usher" by Edgar Allan Poe. What are some of the reasons why authors might use this technique?

- Investigate the dictates of Puritan culture. How is contemporary American culture different? How is it the same?

- What effects did the Salem Witch Trials have on the nation as a whole? Cite specific historic examples.

Guilt vs. Innocence

Hawthorne presents Young Goodman Brown's evening of diabolical revelry as the first and last fling with evil the inexperienced young man ever has. Early in the story, Brown says: "after this one night I'll cling to [Faith's] skirts and follow her to heaven." He believes Faith is an "angel" and one of the Puritan elect who is destined for heaven.

Unfortunately, Brown's experience in the forest makes him reject his previous conviction of the prevailing power of good. He instead embraces the Devil's claim—"Evil is the nature of mankind"— by crying out "Come, devil: for to thee is this world given." This acknowledgment, fueled by the discovery of hypocrisy in the catechist, clergy, the magistrates of Salem, and his own wife, destroys Brown's faith in the Puritan elect. It also sets the tone for the rest of his life. Critics often view this outcome as an attack by Hawthorne on the unredemptive nature of the Puritan belief system, which holds that people are evil by nature because of original sin.

Alienation vs. Community

Though Brown successfully rejects the Devil in his physical form, he allows sin to reside within him when he rejects his belief in humanity. "Often, awakening suddenly at midnight, he shrank from the bosom of Faith, and at morning or eventide, when the family knelt down at prayer, he scowled, and muttered to himself, and gazed at his wife, and turned away." By turning away, Brown becomes the symbolic representation of Hawthorne's belief in the isolation of the human spirit. In Hawthorne's own words, every human being is alone "in that saddest of all prisons, his own heart."

Good vs. Evil

In "Young Goodman Brown," Hawthorne presents sin as an inescapable part of human nature. The fact that Goodman Brown only has to make his journey into the evil forest once suggests that the spiritual quest is a ritual all humans must undergo at some point in their lives. Brown, however, proves himself incapable of accepting this part of the human condition and cannot move forward with his life as a result.

Faith, on the other hand, makes a leap of love and faith to welcome her husband back with open arms from his inexplicable night away from home. Brown, however, "looks sadly and sternly into her face and passes without greeting." Whereas Faith is able to accept the inevitable fallen nature of humanity and live prosperously with this realization, Brown the absolutist cannot accept this truth, and remains stuck in a state of suspicion and ill feelings. By portraying these two reactions, Hawthorne makes a statement not only about the black-and-white, Puritan view of good and evil, but how evil can take other forms as well.

"Young Goodman Brown" tells the tale of a young Puritan man drawn into a covenant with the Devil, which he adamantly tries to resist. His illusions about the goodness of society are crushed when he discovers that many of his fellow townspeople, including religious leaders and his wife, are attending the same Black Mass.

Allegory

"Young Goodman Brown" takes the form of an allegory. An allegory uses symbolic elements to represent various human characteristics and situations. Brown represents Everyman ("Goodman" was a title for those under the social rank of "gentleman") while Faith represents his faith in humanity and society. In leaving his wife, Brown forsakes his belief in the godliness of humanity. He immediately enters a wood "lonely as could be" that is enshrouded in a "deep dusk." These woods are the physical location in which Brown explores his doubts and opposing desires, and as such represent his personal hell. When he tells his companion "Faith kept me back awhile," it is clear that he feels ambivalent about forging a pact with the Devil. Yet, while Brown pledges to return to Faith several times, he continues his dark journey. Although Brown eventually leaves the physical location of the woods, mentally he stays there for the rest of his life.

Symbolism

Examples of symbolism in "Young Goodman Brown" include the pink hair ribbons, which represent Faith's innocence, and the snake-like staff, which is symbolic of the form the Devil takes to corrupt Adam and Eve in the Bible. Another symbol emphasizes a reaction instead of an object. The example unfolds part way through Brown's journey into the woods, immediately after he recognizes the voices of the deacon and the minister. The narrator relates that "Young Goodman Brown caught hold of a tree for support, being ready to sink down on the ground, faint and overburdened with the heavy sickness of his heart." This action symbolizes Brown's wavering faith and his growing realization that he is losing his basis of moral support.

Point of View

Throughout "Young Goodman Brown" point-of-view swings subtly between the narrator and the title character. As a result, readers are privy to Goodman Brown's deepest, darkest thoughts, while also receiving an objective view of his behavior. Early in the story readers learn from Brown himself that he expects his journey to be a one-time event: "Well, [Faith is] a blessed angel on earth; and after this one night I'll cling to her skirts and follow her to heaven." In contrast, readers get an intriguing perspective on Brown's mad dash to the Devil's altar from the objective narrator: "The whole forest was peopled with frightful sounds. . . . But he was himself the chief horror of the scene, and shrank not from its other horrors." By the end of the story, the narrator supplies the only point of view; Brown's voice is conspicuously absent. This shift symbolizes the loss of Brown's faith.

Foreshadowing

Hawthorne uses foreshadowing to build suspense and offer clues as to the story's direction. As Brown leaves for his mysterious journey, Faith voices her doubts: "Prithee put off your journey until sunrise and sleep in your own bed tonight. A lone woman is troubled with dreams and such thoughts that she's afeared of herself sometimes." This statement predicts Faith's betrayal and her appearance at the Black Mass. Brown offers a second example of foreshadowing during a brief monologue: "What a wretch I am to leave her on such an errand. . . . Methought as she spoke there was trouble in her face, as if a dream had warned her what work is to be done tonight. But no, no; 't would kill her to think it." Here Hawthorne hints both at Brown's later confusion over whether he had dreamed his experience and the symbolic death of Faith's innocence at the Black Mass.

Romanticism

Romanticism was a literary movement

originating in the eighteenth century that emphasized imagination and emotion, yet it was also marked by sensibility and autobiographical elements. According to *Compton's Interactive Encyclopedia*, Romanticists held that absolute principles lead to personal failure. Based on the destiny of the title character, it is clear Hawthorne subscribes to this theory as well. Unable to accept the duality of human nature—that good and evil can and often do exist side by side—Goodman Brown lives out the rest of his days as "a stern, a sad, a darkly meditative, a distrustful, if not a desperate man."

Other examples of the Romanticist at work include an underlying message in "Young Goodman Brown" that urges readers to examine the effect their behavior has on others and to change accordingly. This message illustrates the Romanticist conviction that human nature can change for the better.

Lingering Puritan Influences in Nineteenth-Century New England

Although the Salem Witch Trials had unfolded more than one hundred years prior, nineteenth-century New England was still reeling from inherited guilt, even as it rebelled against the constrictive morals of its forebears, the Puritans. It was into this Salem, Massachusetts, society that Hawthorne was born in 1804. Despite the fact he listed Unitarian as his official religion, his roots and sensibilities were unmistakably Puritan.

Hawthorne's great, great grandfather William Hathorne (Nathaniel added the "W" to the family name when he began signing his published works) was the first family member to emigrate from England. He once ordered the public whipping of a Quaker woman who refused to renounce her religious beliefs. Following in the footsteps of his father, William's son, John, presided over the Salem Witch Trials. Hawthorne claims he was frequently haunted by these unholy ghosts from his past. Hawthorne's heritage was not the sole influence on his development, however; the social tenets of his contemporary society also played a key role.

Nineteenth-century English traveler Thomas Hamilton once described the descendants of New

England's first colonists as "cold, shrewd, calculating and ingenious," and asserted that "a New Englander is far more a being of reason than of impulse." Hawthorne applied these traits and values —which he struggled to accept within himself—to his characters, including the title character in "Young Goodman Brown." According to Hyatt H. Waggoner in his book, *Nathaniel Hawthorne*, Hawthorne "continued to note in himself, and to disapprove, feelings and attitudes he projected in. . . Young Goodman Brown. He noted his tendency not only to study others with cool objectivity, but to study himself with almost obsessive interest." The same Puritan values that inspired Hawthorne's objective observation of people and events contributed to his growth and genius as a writer.

At least one other classically Puritan trait emerges in Hawthorne's writings: a keen interest in the welfare of the community. With its emphasis on brotherhood and the perils of alienation, "Young Goodman Brown" is a good example of a Puritan society. "Salem was a part of him," Waggoner concluded, "for good and ill."

Compare & Contrast

- **1692:** The Salem Witch Trials result in the hanging deaths of nineteen people accused of being witches.

  1835: Hawthorne, a descendant of one of the judges who presided over the Witch Trials, publishes "Young

Goodman Brown." The allegorical tale explores the society and the mindset that spawned the trials.

1996: Arthur Miller's play, *The Crucible*, is adapted for film. In 1953 Miller's play used the Salem Witch Trials as an allegory to condemn the actions of Sen. Joseph McCarthy's House Un-American Activities Committee.

- **1690:** The first newspaper in British North America. *Publick Occurrences Both Foreign and Domestick*, is established. The Governor of Massachusetts scuttles the paper before the end of the year.

1835: James Gordon Bennett opens the *New York Herald*. Six years later, the *New York Tribune* is founded. These papers, which cost one penny, are meant to reach the multitudes and be non-partisan.

1997: *USA Today* is the nation's leading newspaper, based on circulation figures. Founded in 1982, it is the first paper to be published at several printing plants throughout the nation simultaneously.

- **1600s:** The Native American population numbers an estimated six to nine million.

1800s: The Native American population numbers less than three million.

1997: The Native American population (now including Eskimo and Aleut ethnicities) has recently risen to just over two million.

The Industrial Revolution and the Publishing Business

Printed communication increased by leaps and bounds in the first half of the nineteenth century as a result of new technology. Publishers enlarged their size and scope under the pressure of competition, and new agencies of delivery—including the ocean steamship and the railroad—increased the speed and efficiency of publishing. Improved presses sped up the rate of printing twenty-fold between 1830 and 1850. This trend contributed to Hawthorne's public reputation and income as many of his earlier short stories and essays found their way into print via a newsman's press.

The literary output of New England writers between 1830 and 1850 was not only noteworthy for its volume but also because it reflected the qualities of the region, new contacts with European culture, and the spirit of Jacksonian Democracy. The works of many writers of this period—

including Oliver Wendell Holmes, Herman Melville, and Edgar Allan Poe—are still widely read today. According to Frederick Jackson Turner in his book *The United States, 1830-1850: The Nation and Its Sections*, however, Hawthorne was "the greatest of the New England novelists" and exhibited "a power of psychological analysis and literary skill that have not since been equaled by any American writer."

Critical Overview

From the publication of his first collection of stories, *Twice Told Tales*, Hawthorne's books were reviewed often and enthusiastically. Although lavishly praised by critics, the collection itself sold poorly; an enlarged edition issued in 1842 fared no better. This pattern of critical appreciation and public neglect continued throughout Hawthorne's literary career, and he was forced to occupy a series of minor governmental posts in order to supplement his income. Hawthorne's work, which consists of over fifty stories and sketches as well as such classic novels as *The Scarlet Letter*, has continuously drawn critical and popular attention since his death. His work draws readers not only for its strong storytelling qualities but also for the moral and theological questions raised within.

"Young Goodman Brown" ranks foremost among Hawthorne's short stories in both popular appeal and critical respect. It remains a favorite because it holds something of interest for almost everyone, be it plot line, the title character's moral dilemma, or the tale's ambiguity. Yet this universal appeal comes not at any sacrifice of artistic or structural integrity.

Some notable American authors of the nineteenth century, however, dismissed "Young Goodman Brown" for its strong allegorical structure. Edgar Allan Poe thought Hawthorne's use of allegory distracted from the natural elements of his work, while Henry James believed it constituted Hawthorne's propsenity for taking the easy way out. Of Hawthorne's contemporaries, only Herman Melville saw merit in "Young Goodman Brown." "Who in the name of thunder," Melville wrote in *Nathaniel Hawthorne's Tales*, "would anticipate any marvel in a piece entitled 'Young Goodman Brown?' You would of course suppose that it was a simple little tale, intended as a supplement to 'Goody Two-Shoes.' Whereas it is deep as Dante."

Over the years, critics came to agree with Melville rather than Poe and James. In 1945, Richard H. Fogle offered these words of tribute in *New England Quarterly:* "In 'Young Goodman Brown,' then, Hawthorne has achieved that reconciliation of opposites which [Samuel Taylor] Coleridge deemed the highest art. The combination of clarity of technique, embodied in simplicity and balance of structure, in firm pictorial composition, in contrast and climactic arrangement, in irony and detachment, with ambiguity of meaning as signalized by the device of multiple choice, in its interrelationships produces the story's characteristic effect." Nearly twenty years later, critic David Levin was still finding genius in Hawthorne's outwardly simple tale. "By recognizing that Hawthorne built 'Young Goodman Brown' firmly on his historical knowledge," Levin wrote in *American Literature*, "we perceive that the tale has a social as well as an allegorical and psychological dimension."

Sources

Fogle, Richard H. "Ambiguity and Clarity in Hawthorne's 'Young Goodman Brown'," in *New England Quarterly*, December, 1945.

Levin, David in *American Literature*, November, 1962.

Melville, Herman. "Hawthorne and His Mosses," in *Nathaniel Hawthorne's Tales*, edited by James McIntosh, W. W. Norton, 1987, pp. 337-350.

Poe, Edgar Allan. "Tale-Writing—Nathaniel Hawthorne," in *Nathaniel Hawthorne's Tales*, edited by James McIntosh, W. W. Norton, 1987.

Turner, Frederick Jackson. *The United States, 1830-1850: The Nation and Its Sections*, Peter Smith, 1958.

Waggoner, Hyatt H. *Nathaniel Hawthorne*, University of Minnesota Press, 1962, 48 p.

Further Reading

Levy, Leo B. "The Problem of Faith in 'Young Goodman Brown'," in *Nathaniel Hawthorne*, edited by Harold Bloom, Chelsea House, 1986, pp. 115-26.

> Levy discusses some of the critical interpretations of "Young Goodman Brown" and provides his own reading of the story, focusing on the character of Faith.

Newman, Lea Bertani Vozar. *A Reader's Guide to the Short Stories of Nathaniel Hawthorne*, G. K. Hall & Co., 1979.

> Newman covers all of Hawthorne's stories, presenting publication history, circumstances of composition, sources, influences, relationships with other Hawthorne works, and interpretations and criticisms.

St. Armand, Barton Levi. "'Young Goodman Brown' as Historical Allegory," in *Nathaniel Hawthorne Journal*, 1973, pp. 183-97.

> St. Armand presents a discussion of "Young Goodman Brown" as allegory and provides references to the Puritan background of the story's setting.

Lightning Source UK Ltd.
Milton Keynes UK
UKHW020937160223
417123UK00006B/577